Songs of Myself

An Anthology of Poems and Art

Compiled by Georgia Heard

To Leo—the true song of myself
—G. H.

Acknowledgments

Special thanks to Artemis Picture Research Group, Inc., and to Ann Sandhorst for their invaluable help.

The Lawrence Tree by Georgia O'Keeffe. WADSWORTH ATHENEUM, HARTFORD. The Ella Gallup Sumner and Mary Catlin Sumner Collection Fund. Copyright © 2000 The Georgia O'Keeffe Foundation / Artists Rights Society (ARS), New York.

"Every Morning" by George Swede. Copyright © George Swede. Used by permission of the author.

Running House / #4862 by Nicholas Wilton. Used by permission of the artist.

"By Myself," from HONEY, I LOVE by Eloise Greenfield. Text copyright © 1978 by Eloise Greenfield. Used by permission of HarperCollins Publishers.

Korean Child, 1958 by Dorothea Lange. Copyright the Dorothea Lange Collection, the Oakland Museum of California, City of Oakland. Gift of Paul S. Taylor.

"Everybody Says," from HERE, THERE, AND EVERYWHERE by Dorothy Aldis. Copyright © 1927, 1928, copyright renewed © 1955, 1956 by Dorothy Aldis. Used by permission of G. P. Putnam's Sons, a division of Penguin Putnam, Inc.

Elsie Cassatt Holding a Big Dog by Mary Cassatt. Copyright © Christie's Images.

"The Voice" from FALLING UP by Shel Silverstein. Copyright © 1996 by Shel Silverstein. Used by permission of HarperCollins Publishers.

Echoes of Harlem by Faith Ringgold. Collection, Philip Morris Companies, Inc., and copyright © 1980 Faith Ringgold.

"Orders," by A. M. Klein, from 'TIL ALL THE STARS HAVE FALLEN, selected by David Booth. First published in Canada by Kids Can Press, Ltd., 1989. First published in the U.S. by Viking, 1990.

Adventurers Between Adventures by Norman Rockwell. Copyright © Brown & Bigelow, Inc.

"My Horse and I," by Georgia Heard. Copyright © 2000 by Georgia Heard.

Sky Ride by Janîce Leotti. Copyright © 2000. Used by permission of the artist.

WHAT IT IS by Nellie Mae Rowe. Collection of Judith Alexander. Photograph courtesy of the Museum of American Folk Art.

"Running Away," from NEAR THE WINDOW TREE by Karla Kuskin. Copyright © 1975 by Karla Kuskin. Text reprinted by permission of Scott Treimel New York.

"I Have All These Parts . . ." from ALL THE COLORS OF THE RACE by Arnold Adoff. Copyright © 1982 by Arnold Adoff, Lothrop, Lee & Shepard Books.

Photo illustration by Jay Corbett used by permission of the artist.

"the drum," from SPIN A SOFT BLACK SONG, REVISED EDITION by Nikki Giovanni. Copyright © 1971, 1985 by Nikki Giovanni. Reprinted by permission of Farrar, Straus and Giroux, LLC.

World Drum by Brad Teare, Artworks Illustration, NY. Used by permission of the artist.

Cut-paper sculpture by Meredith Thomas. Used by permission of the artist. Photographed by David Ascoli.

"The First Day of Spring," from FRESH PAINT by Eve Merriam. Copyright © 1986 Eve Merriam. Used by permission of Marian Reiner.

"Who Am I?" from AT THE TOP OF MY VOICE AND OTHER POEMS by Felice Holman. Copyright © 1971, published by Charles Scribner's Sons. Used by permission of Felice Holman.

Amanda, painting by Judy Pedersen. Used by permission of the artist.

Number 8 by Mark Rothko. Copyright © Christie's Images.

Arrangement for "This Little Light of Mine" by John Zaccari.

Every effort has been made to trace the ownership of all copyrighted materials in this book and to obtain permission for their use.

For information contact:
MONDO Publishing
980 Avenue of the Americas
New York, NY 10018

Designed by David Neuhaus/NeuStudio
Production by The Kids at Our House
Printed by Phoenix Color Corp.

Library of Congress Cataloging-in-Publication Data available upon request.
ISBN 1-57255-723-0 (hardcover) — ISBN 1-57255-854-7 (big book) — ISBN 1-57255-722-2 (pbk.)
Printed in the United States of America

00 01 02 03 04 05 06 07   HC   9 8 7 6 5 4 3 2 1
00 01 02 03 04 05 06 07   PB   9 8 7 6 5 4 3 2 1

Contents

Introduction

"I celebrate myself and sing myself . . ." is how the famous poet Walt Whitman began his long poem *Song of Myself*. This poem inspired me to create this anthology. I chose the poems and art in this book to help us celebrate and explore the many different parts of ourselves.

During the course of a day, or a week, or a year, we have many different moods, thoughts, and feelings. In fact, within each one of us, there isn't just one self but many selves. For example, we have a "by myself" self, the person we are when we are alone; or a self when we have a lot of chores or obligations ahead of us—a self that just wants to run away and go play; or a self that stands under a starry night, feels so small, and asks the question, "Who am I?" All of these varying parts help to make us the unique individuals that we are.

Poetry and art are mirrors of the self—that's why they sometimes help us to see and celebrate our lives and ourselves in new ways. The art I chose represents a range of American artists and illustrators, from the famous woman artist Mary Cassatt, who painted a long time ago, to more modern artists and illustrators who are still creating today. The poems I chose also vary—from William Shakespeare to Shel Silverstein.

At first glance, you may not see yourself in a particular poem or picture, but if you look again and look closely, you will be able to find a part of yourself in every poem and picture in this anthology. So, I invite you to read the poems and gaze at the sampling of art—and to keep asking yourself that important question, "Who am I?"

Georgia Heard

The Lawrence Tree
  Georgia O'Keeffe
  oil on canvas

A star danced
and under that
was I born.

William Shakespeare

Every Morning

Every morning
I awake
full of dust
and odors

As if
no one has
lived in me
for years

And
every morning
I throw open
all my windows
and doors

Clean
and fumigate
myself

As if
I were just
moving in

George Swede

Running House / #4862
 Nicholas Wilton
 oil on corrugated cardboard

By Myself

When I'm by myself
And I close my eyes
I'm a twin
I'm a dimple in a chin
I'm a room full of toys
I'm a squeaky noise
I'm a gospel song
I'm a gong
I'm a leaf turning red
I'm a loaf of brown bread
I'm a whatever I want to be
An anything I care to be
And when I open my eyes
What I care to be
Is me

Eloise Greenfield

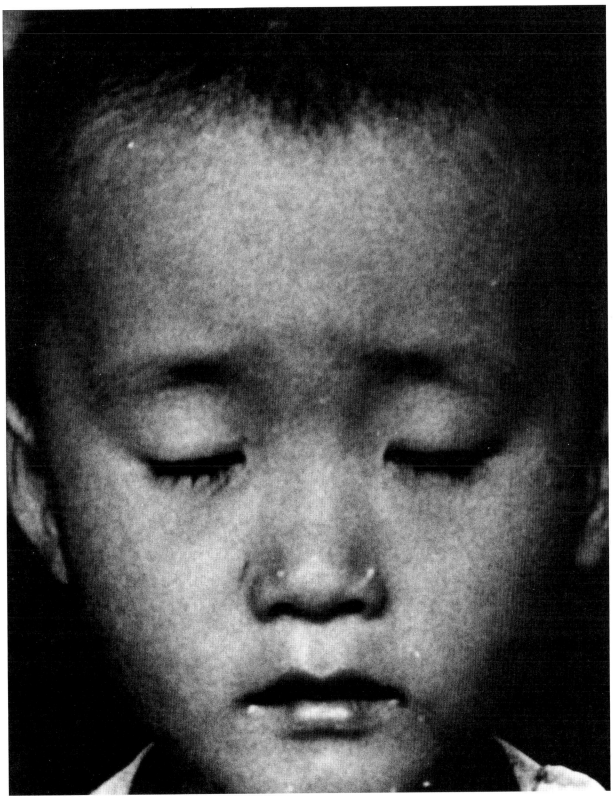

Korean Child, 1958
   Dorothea Lange
   8″ x 10″ black and white print

Everybody Says

Everybody says
I look just like my mother.
Everybody says
I'm the image of Aunt Bee.
Everybody says
My nose is like my father's,
But *I* want to look like *me*.

Dorothy Aldis

The Voice

There is a voice inside of you
That whispers all day long,
"I feel that this is right for me,
I know that *this* is wrong."
No teacher, preacher, parent, friend
Or wise man can decide
What's right for you — just listen to
The voice that speaks inside.

Shel Silverstein

Echoes of Harlem, 1980
   Faith Ringgold / W. Possi
   hand-painted cotton, 100" x 96"

Orders

Muffle the wind;
Silence the clock;
Muzzle the mice;
Curb the small talk;
Cure the hinge-squeak;
Banish the thunder.
Let me sit silent,
Let me wonder.

A. M. Klein

Adventurers Between Adventures
Norman Rockwell

My Horse and I *(poem for two voices)*

We gallop

	We gallop
Together	
	Together
	Over the hills
Across the fields	
	Follow the creek
Who is the girl?	
	Who is the horse?
I am the girl	I am the horse
I am the horse	I am the girl
We gallop	
	We gallop
Together	Together
Together	Together

Georgia Heard

Sky Ride
Janîce Leotti
oil on board

WHAT IT IS
 Nellie Mae Rowe
 Atlanta, Georgia
 1981

Running Away

Running away
From the rest of today
Running away
From you
Running away
From "Don't do that"
From all of the things
I must constantly do.
I feel too tall
I feel too old
For a hundred helpings of being told.
Packing my head
Taking my feet
Galloping down the familiar street.
My head is a bird.
My heart is free again.
I might come back
When I feel like me again.

Karla Kuskin

I Have All These Parts . . .

I have all these parts stuffed in
                              me
like mama's chicken
            and
            biscuits,
            and
daddy's apple pie, and a tasty
                        story
from the family
            tree.

But I know that tomorrow
                  morning
      I'll wake up
            empty, and hungry for that
                              next
                              bite
      of my new
            day.

Arnold Adoff

Jay Corbett
photo illustration

the drum

Daddy says the world is
a drum tight and hard
and I told him
i'm gonna beat
out my own rhythm.

Nikki Giovanni

World Drum
Brad Teare
scratchboard

The First Day of Spring

The first day of spring
itches
because
an emerald blade of grass
is
pushing out
of
my forehead

I've become
a unicorn.

Eve Merriam

Cut-paper sculpture
Meredith Thomas
Photographed by David Ascoli

Who Am I?

The trees ask me,
And the sky,
And the sea asks me
Who am I?

The grass asks me,
And the sand,
And the rocks ask me
Who I am.

The wind tells me
At nightfall,
And the rain tells me
Someone small.

Someone small
Someone small
But a piece
of
it
all.

Felice Holman

This Little Light of Mine

(Chorus)
This little light of mine, I'm gonna let it shine.
This little light of mine, I'm gonna let it shine.
This little light of mine, I'm gonna let it shine,
Ev'ry day, ev'ry day, ev'ry day.
Gonna let my little light shine.

On Monday, gave me the gift of love,
Tuesday peace came from above,
Wednesday told me to have more faith,
Thursday gave me a little grace,
Friday sat me down to pray,
Saturday told me what to say,
Sunday gave me the power divine
just to let my little light shine.

The light that shines is the light of love,
Lights the darkness from above.
It shines on me and it shines on you,
Shows what the power of love can do.

Traditional song

Number 8
    Mark Rothko
    1903-1970
    Signed, numbered, and dated 1952 on reverse
    oil on canvas
    $80\frac{3}{4}'' \times 68\frac{1}{8}''$

This Little Light of Mine

Traditional
Arranged by John Zacca

Moderately